Ark Music
Sue Boyle

by the same author

TOO LATE FOR THE LOVE HOTEL

ON BOARD ARCADIA
Volume One: A Day Out on the Thames
Volume Two: Mr Marksbury's Careful Choice of Beds
Volume Three: A Respectable Neighbourhood
Volume Four: Report from the Judenplatz
Volume Five: Ark Music

Sue Boyle

ARK MUSIC

Time & Tide Publishing
London EC1

Published by Time & Tide Publishing 2013
London EC1

© Sue Boyle 2013

COVER
Night Fishing
Watercolour by an unknown artist c. 1830

ISBN-13:978-1491041772

A CIP catalogue record for this book
is available from the British Library.

All rights reserved. No part of this publication
may be reproduced in any form or by any means
(electronic, mechanical, photocopying, recording or otherwise)
without the prior written permission of both the copyright owner
and the publisher of this book.

timeandtidepublishing@gmail.com

*What is man
that thou art mindful of him?
and the sonne of man
that thou visitest him?*

*For thou hast made him
a little lower than the Angels;
and hast crowned him
with glory and honour.*

*Thou madest him
to have dominion
over the works of thy hands;
thou hast put all things
under his feete.*

*All sheepe and oxen, yea
and the beasts of the field.*

*The foule of the aire,
and the fish of the sea,
and whatsoever passeth
through the paths of the seas.*

*O Lord our Lord,
how excellent is thy name
in all the earth.*

Psalm Eight
verses 3–9

contents

evolution 1
the seafarer 2
missing at sea 3
candles for the kursk 4
the roman soldier 5
the questions we could not ask 6
stone considers its place 7
earthquake 8
terremoto 9
the field of miracles 10
pietà 11
safe passage 12
the death of the emperor 13
homer 14
lost 15
the village volunteers 16 & 17
the loss 18
old cat 19
the others 19
high table 20
birthsong 21
ark music 22
restored 24
new year 25
he tells them stories 26
the new ark 27

Acknowledgements 29
About the author 30
On Board Arcadia 30

evolution

Tiktaalik roseae – though he must wait
375 million years to learn his name –
nudged at the glassy membrane
which ceilinged his wet world
and imagined in his ambitious
but meagre brain
sanctuary from his appalling predators,
the beatitude of angels, unrefracted
sunshine, the end of toil.

Hungry, he nudged again,
pushed, punctured, flexed his fins,
eager to possess his bright new home.
Blunt-nosed and clumsy,
he had the idea to fly,
look down from an exalted height,
destroy his enemies by fire
and glory in the blessing
of the gods.

the seafarer

A man, his axe, a tree in sight of water;
an idea to be unconfined,
not to give in to the unknown.
He finds that oak can be felled,
planked, bowed into new shapes;
that a man can impose his will
to make water's plough.

Now ocean is his province like the earth.

He names the winds, the archipelagos,
their bounty of living things;
takes oyster for the improbable prize of pearl;
ransacks the whale;
devours the distances in search of war.
On the seabed his bones,
rocked and imprisoned by water,
imagine the voyage home.

missing at sea

Toll out who sailed, what ships they sailed, their names –
the Saxon Monarch, Jacob Rickinson.
Land gave them life: the sea took it away.

These little seaboys swallowed by the waves –
Jelson Cornforth, Isaac Miles Harrison.
Toll out who sailed, what ships they sailed, their names.

These master mariners who could not save
their ships – Henry Streeting, Thomas Hewson.
Land gave them life: the sea took it away.

In oceans' hunger and wars' wild affrays –
Steamship Bagdale, Steamship Hollington.
Toll out who sailed, what ships they sailed, their names.

Recite his litany across the bay –
from brig Miranda, Robert Parkinson.
Land gave him life: the sea took it away.

Till seas return their dead on Judgment Day –
King's Ship Sutherland, Thomas Allotson.
Toll out who sailed, what ships they sailed, their names.
Land gave them life: the sea took it away.

from the archive of Storm and Company, Robin Hood's Bay

candles for the kursk

Who knows what was lost
when the sea took charge of them?
Who knew them enough to say,
Ignore his name, his rank.
This was the man he was.

Sergei's son, the virgin Nikolai,
black toothed and garlic breathed –
an acrobat in Omsk once looked his way.
Unless with that speechless
airy, supple, spangled girl,
he wanted no truck with love.

Some waited hours, a few waited
days to die. When each is his own
darkness, his memory scrolling,
flickering to its end,
who knows the mystery, terrors,
blisspoints of his years?

This for Vasily, Anya's favourite son,
student of orchids, shore leave stargazer,
who laughed and drank too much
and slept too lightly
afraid in a deeper sleep he might dream again
the black, the mass and patience of the water.

Barents Sea, August 2000

the roman soldier
explains things to his son

Beyond a certain point we believe
that a fallen body is not sensible
so we will not experience earth's
tidy and purposeful depredations –
the tap touch of its insects,
the probe of mandibles
or, in the case of a drowning,
the enquiries of little fish,
the resolve of battening eels.

Whatever the case, nothing to fear
is the way you must think of this.
We expect not pain, but a sense of wonderment
as the body passes itself into the fabric
of these thousand lives of which before
it had lived in ignorance.

Who becomes an ant
becomes one of the world's most admired minutiae;
who becomes a fish
will be as astonished as one who travels to the moon;
as a worm, the womb of the earth
will be open to him again;
as a bird, he will master the over-arching sky.

It does them no favours, the pomp
and circumstance we accord our generals –
the orations, the wailing women, the catafalques.

The dead make their own way to immortality.

Return to earth is the way to think of this.

the questions
we could not ask

When our enemies cut logs for their winters,
did they use the same tools as my father did –
bowsaw, sawbench, chopping block, small axe?
Were our enemies and their children as beguiled
by the unexpected fidgets and frets of severed wood,
the surprise of its inner life?

The hiss of escaping sap, the ooze and bleed
of resin from wood's heart –
did our enemies' children read
the same legends of dissolution on their hearths?
The cities on furious fire, the scorch, the glow,
the encroach of the ambient dark?

Those streamlined exits
from silo and water, their shallow arcs
on the fields of black space
below the bewildered stars,
their cunning tilts round the turning earth –
did our enemies' children know
what my father was forbidden to tell us –

that somewhere above the Pole
the contrary flightpaths would cross
and armageddon be unstoppable
thanks to men like him
whose job was to tend the fires
at home, and at work to engineer
nuclear missiles' pinpoint homings in?

stone considers its place
in the scheme of things

one
What the lizards do is bask
their belly sacs, their crepey slacks of throat
on my weathered skin. They have old, cold hearts
and need the heat I borrow from the sun.

The whales who season by season have to track
across me through vasts of water, sing
down for safe passage.
Echo is the blessing I send back.

Fierce eagles take advantage of my height
to plummet for prey. I ledge their screaming young.
Light as cloudshadow on me are these lives
except for late-comer, man, whose iron bite
breaks me to build walls.

This two-legged creature of chisel,
delve and hack is no historian –
scratching his name on slabs of plundered stone,
thinking no empire will outlast his own.

two
My scale is beyond his brain.
Continents come apart if it is my wish.
Earthquake is one of my weapons.
I am also adamantine. I can wait.

earthquake

If all these holy places,
with their confidence
and genius of making –
San Francesco, San Paulo,
Santa Caterina, Sant' Antonio –
If all these churches built to praise
the Greatest of all the Makers –

If even these

can fail

become rubble, splinter, dust

so frail which seemed so strong

so friable –

If these, then what of us
cast out imperfect,
from that same Great Maker's Garden,
dear friend, then what of us?

Emilia-Romagna, May 2012
For G.C.

terremoto

Se questi luoghi benedetti,
con tutta la loro intimità
e genialità creativa;
San Francesco, San Paolo
Santa Caterina, Sant'Antonio.
Se tutte queste chiese costruite in lode
del più Grande degli Autori,
se perfino queste
possono cadere,
divenire macerie, frammenti, polvere,
se è così gracile ciò che sembrava robusto
e così friabile,
se anche il prediletto può franare,
cosa dire di noi, isolati nella nostra imperfezione,
esuli dal Suo Giardino, caro amico,
cosa dire di noi?

Emilia-Romagna, maggio 2012
trans. Giancarlo Caine
Sacile 2012

the field of miracles

Each summer in the garden is the same –
the year's young colony of frogs
as sudden in their leaps as grasshoppers,
no larger than enlivened pumpkin seeds,
scrabble the margin for better vantage,
each other's bodies their soft stepping stones.
Compelled to a dazzling unfamiliar world,
most of them will never see the spring.

And each year in the city is the same –
the Drop Dead Gorgeous girls hen partying,
giggling their secrets, practising new heels,
who vanish in a glide of limousine
to matings from which some of them emerge
these burdened harassed mothers on the bus
with anxious children, tired trainers,
too much mouth and jumbo bags of crisps.

*How snugly the meadow pipit fits
the merlin's foot.*

                          Life feeds itself
on the shipwreck of its dear creatures.
For us no day was ever long enough –
Pisa at dawn, the Field of Miracles,
Lucca, the Corso Garibaldi, the magnolias –
while someone we loved waited
without hope in her far country.

That butterfly garden.

Captive white peacocks dancing in the sun.

Quotation from Michael Longley's 'Call'
A Hundred Doors, *2011*

pietà

The actresses from the burlesque theatre
have changed from their working clothes
to join the crowds on the pavement
who have gathered to watch
the important procession as it passes by.

Surrounding the popemobile,
dark-suited bodyguards, helmeted outriders,
men with walkie-talkies, armed police.

Now, from the hospices, care homes, hospitals,
on their crutches, in their wheelchairs, on their beds,
each with a priest or a crisply laundered nun,
the worn-out, injured, fragile, ailing ones
struggle their own slow progress up the street.

Some, as if celebrities for one day,
give us the gracious papal nod and wave.
Some smile. Some cannot smile. Some laugh
as though we wrong-footed motley onlookers
were actors in a lost comedic world.

We do not jostle now, nor photograph.
Clapping and waving fail as each attends
the sorrow and compassion in himself –
a communion of faithless and faithful,
of watchers and the watched.

Feast of the Immaculate Conception
Via Dei Due Macelli, Rome

safe passage

The oculus in the bridge
gives warning that the Tiber
is on the brink of flood.

Thanks to Pope Sixtus and his architect,
the handbag sellers, pampered little dogs,
bravado boys who perch the parapet
and tiny Genghis Khan with his violin
are safe. However high the water,
to and from Trastevere,
providing the island
can be seen through the oculus,
the life of the bridge goes on.

If the eye were blinded by water
it would be time to leave
but who can leave himself?

Not poor John Clare,
the torrent of voices roaring in his head,
nor in their babels, bedlams,
in their fearful rooms,
Janey, Eliza, William, Christopher,
their minds' foundations shifting in the flood,
not these who cry out but none
can rescue from themselves –

as if the drowned could cry for help,
fathoms already down
a mountain of blind water.

Ponte Sisto, Rome

the death of the emperor

He is all his selves now and he is none.
He is feared and loved: they are awed and curious.
Nothing will be the same: nothing will change.
He is not replaceable: has already been replaced.
He is all his truths: he is none of them
and never was.

Along his northern wall
his soldiers hear the news
and say in their cups,
the emperor was such and such,
or thus and so,
what will become of us?
will they call us home?

Kites hover in his skies; the fox and wolf
hunt as they always have; women as usual long
to be loved by the worst of men.
Sheep wool snagged on thorn;
a half moon in clear sky above the hills
and he who owned it all, indifferent now,
being all his selves, and being none of them.

Hadrian's Mausoleum, Rome

homer

He envied their strange
satisfaction with surfaces,
how they loved to hear
about the hero Achilles
buckling his bronze greaves,
the gleaming shields,
the gorgeous chariots.

He envied their fantasy
that these accomplished
killers were not themselves
writ simpler and writ large,
their fiction that it was the fault
of squabbling invented gods.

Hector of the glittering helmet,
Diomed tamer of horses,
Odysseus the all-daring
the illustrious.

Only the singer heard
the undersong in his own tall tales –
the later and lesser men
who would ebb and flow
as if trapped forever
on that windy plain

their cities unbuilt
but already burning,
their generations
unborn but already seeking
return to the earth again.

lost

Remember my uncle John
who closed this Chiswick door
that June in the early morning
and stepped out smartly
for Paddington Station
from where he was conveyed
by troop train to Torquay
in convoy to Bulawayo
and last by plane
to the western deserts
of North Africa above which
he would soon fall
spiralling and burning
a thing that would never
on any day be mentioned
nor for any half hour forgotten
by my grandfather
who in the spring of 1943
had no greater designs
for himself and his son
than for the two of them
to cross London
on their matching
Raleigh bicycles
to see West Ham play again
at Upton Park and secure
another decisive victory
over their arch rivals Millwall
those elegant devilish players
from the terrible Isle of Dogs.

the village volunteers

Thomas Adlard, October 1916

On the day he brought the two huge horses
down for the last time from the top field,
did he know what would stay with him?
His village already estranging itself in dark;
another train clanking south; rooks clamouring
in the elm trees round the church;
an owl's alert; a fox's early cough;
supper without speech; logs settling on the hearth;
the mantel clock ticking;
how, in the iron bed where they had thought
their children would be born, he lay all night
with his wife uncoupled, held apart –
creatures condemned to the morning
who knew that their time was done.

the village volunteers

Jack Adlard, December 1940

He didn't know when he left the farm
that he'd be the last to work these fields
with the heavy horses; that these two
would be the last to shift and shuffle
in their adjacent stalls in his black barn
and struggle his plough through stony earth;
that the harness would mildew, the brasses dull,
and the blacksmith close his forge for want of these
who stood taller than any man.
Meg and Stranger, solid as two rocks –
Meg sired by Baron out of Amethyst,
Stranger from Amy, sired by Valentine –
both bred at Farrow's Farm
in the lost blue morning of his world
and into what darkness gone.

the loss

After the dealers came for all the horses –
the bays, the roans, the greys, the mares with foals
and the two black hunters, Abel and Joshua –
I did not care to visit Tom Gurney's house.

Three generations our village had been graced
by Gurney horses – Tom's, George his father's,
Owen the grandfather's whose stables sent
their strongest for war service in the same July
my grandfather, Charlie Sladbrook, lost his legs.

It was to fund his divorce that Tom sold off
his horses and their stable block
in the field with the chestnut clumps by Sargeant's mill
which was zoned by the planners later for starter homes,
the barn sold off as a separate lot to a London architect
with a weekend entourage of high-end cars.

Straightbacked riders on their showhorses;
foals gangling on their spring legs;
Tom Gurney's favourite, Dreamer,
practising her steps, alone, in that high field –
her canter, trot, turn on an imagined rein;
the travelling blacksmith, how he talked to them
as he wrenched the old and hammered on
the new shoes; their names, their temperaments,
their histories, their great hooves.

old cat

He sleeps in the weather now:
rain and the wind no longer trouble him.
He lies in mud:
seeds and small slugs insinuate his fur.

He is getting ready,
learning how it works
the turning earth, how it abides,
how small its place in the cage of stars.

When my father stopped speaking
and set aside his shoes it was just like this:
his body sat with us but
his being was no longer in our house.

the others

The children of the less successful gods
did not abuse. Did not incarcerate.
Did nothing to diminish the good earth.
Built no cathedrals. Sent no fellow soul
to sweat and perish down a mine for them.
Their beauty was not painted on.
They gave us athletics, song, good parenting
and left no residue in life except their dung,
in death except the marvel of their bones.

high table

The archaeologist served up a Norfolk goose
whose fat congealed in pools

between our vegetables. 'In Uruguay, we ate
banded armadillo and prairie mice,' he said,

when we could find them. In Panama
last year, we caught a sloth.' 'It isn't hard,'

said his friend, who combed the shards
of ruined Inca cities, 'to catch a sloth.
Like a pretty girl, just hug it and it's yours.

Lizards now are quite a different thing –
fierce little buggers. I always keep the skins –

my boy collects them.' These were men
whom night had not surprised with its net of stars
nor the darkness terrified.

They had eaten oryx, turtle, antelope –
'what bothers me,' said the moral scientist,

carving from an amputated wing,
'are these claims of close kinship –

as if, bar the odd claw and feather,
we were essentially the same.

Homo sapiens is self-aware;
hungers to know the world beyond himself;

to consolidate his knowledge and pass it on.
We are unique in this.' Charles Darwin fixed

small mammals and insects to wooden drawers
with long steel pins for later study in Down House.

Such clever men.
With goose grease on their chins.

birthsong

Let him look through the lens of my unforgiving eye;
let solace of surface be denied to him;
let him see to the deep; let him see to the heart ;
let him see like me, *said pike.*

Cast him beyond all dream;
may what stirs in his sight be moving bones for him;
may his hunger consume unblinking what it sees;
make him like me, *hawk said.*

Warn him how weak he is
who can neither melt to water nor hide to air –
he lacks my devious brain, my rippling guile;
he was born unwise; protect him, *otter said.*

Teach him to fillet sweetness from the years
before love locks deathtight on his tardy heel –
he will need to step high and fast in that bloodred dance
while he runs with a chance,
while his fire flares hot, *said fox.*

ark music

after we had disposed of the zoos
the safari parks, the game reserves,
the david attenborough film archive
and the rain forest experience

we thought that we were safe

that no one would ask the awkward questions any more
because with all the evidence destroyed,
no one would be able to imagine
what awkward questions could be asked

then we noticed how many of the creatures had escaped
and we knew at once who was responsible for this
who it was had left behind
his tremendous baleful requiem
for these others who had always been
so much more central to it all
than most of us had been able to understand

and we also knew that this man's ark music
was going to carry the burden of the remembered names
across the black horror between the galaxies
so that the soaring angels would discover
that these creatures and these only
had been the true princes of the earth

listen they were going to say
hawk, otter, horse, thoughtfox, jaguar
the feathered, the swimming,
the four-footed ones
hear from this man's music
how the earthmen honoured them

and look

on that dying star

a jaguar waiting

the horizons come

restored

One day they will make him marvellous again
the chariot horse whose fragments of statue
wait under this garden laid for a prince.

This oak tree will fall; its tangle of roots reveal
a sculptured eye, the arc of a hoof, the swell
of a polished haunch. It happens here in Rome.

They will replace his armature and speculate,
was this that dangerous tempered horse,
the stallion from the western provinces

who chafed and pawed the sand at the starting gate,
whose nostrils flared so wide at each tight turn
he delighted all of Rome? That legend of a horse

who grazes now
the night-blue meadows of Elysium
and waits for a kindly groom

to bring news that their sorrow is finished;
they can leave the ignoble city;
at last they are going home.

Farnese Gardens, Rome

new year

Across the dark water, dove
looked for her drowned world.
Below and behind her
the ark diminished,
helpless in the grip
of its vengeful, possessive god.

When first light sheened
from the waves, dove thought
of the ubiquitous smell of dung,
the tense exchanges,
the prayers,
the self-importance of the patriarch
and grieved for what was gone.

At second light,
she discovered a new world –
groves on the slopes
of dry mountains; well tilled ground;
pomegranate trees, stately and rich
with their burden of ripe fruit;
birdsong in clean bright air.
She was never going back.

he tells them stories
to see them through

He narrated fish
grilled over charcoal,
succulent, oozing oils,
and bread, new-baked
its warmth still resident;
how these were plentiful;
how no one hungered, none
of that multitude of souls.

Dark howled around them;
mountains hemmed them in;
the valley had no egress.
But his voice was music:
they trusted what he said.
There was kindness among them.
They could not be saved –
but they were comforted.

the new ark

They travelled us in the dark so we had little idea of the direction and distance we might be travelling. We could not read so for the most part we drowsed in our separate worlds of remembering and dreams.

We were each allowed to keep one small animal close to us and to visit the other, larger animals when we chose. I had a sun bear cub on my lap; my companion cradled a white-collared lemur and her eight year old daughter shared her seat with a young iberian lynx. The sense of caring for these non-speaking creatures seemed to relieve us of our personal anxieties and their warmth and childlike affection for us generated a camaraderie throughout our carriage and, I supposed, the train.

I remember that long period of darkness as a happy time. Someone said that the city had fallen and that we must now forget that it had ever been. At one point in our journey the line ran through high mountains whose jagged outlines opened quite suddenly to give a view of an unexpectedly illuminated sea.

A shaft of light drew our attention to an inlet of silver water where we saw a slow procession of unfamiliar animals and birds moving placidly and apparently under no human direction or control two by two up a broad gangway on to a massive barge. Then the bulk of the mountains intervened.

It is for each one of you, said the conductor, to chose to believe whether what you have witnessed is a memory, an illusion, a prophecy or a dream.

acknowledgements

I am very grateful to the editors of *Acumen* and *The Rialto* in which several of these poems first appeared and to Smith/Doorstop for publishing others in *Too Late for the Love Hotel* which was one of the prize-winners in *The North*'s 2010 pamphlet competition judged by the Poet Laureate Andrew Motion.

'Ark Music' and 'The New Ark' were included in a sequence called *Poems for an Endangered Earth* which was written and performed by poets from the Bath Poetry Cafe during the 'Voices in the City' series as part of the Independent Bath Festival of Literature in 2013. I am very grateful to Nikki Kenna, Lesley Saunders, Jill Sharp, Susan Jane Sims and Susan Utting for the opportunity to collaborate with them on this piece.

I am also very grateful to my friend Giancarlo Caine in Sacile for his generosity in letting me use his translation of 'Earthquake' and to Giorgio Piai and Giancarlo Caine for the ongoing pleasure and privilege of seeing and hearing so many of my poems renewed and reinvented in the rhythms and cadences of the beautiful Italian language.

Sue Boyle

L'amore. La morte. How close they are.
The confusion of signs. The fiction of surfaces.

Sue Boyle's *Too Late for the Love Hotel* was a prizewinner in *The North*'s 2010 pamphlet competition judged by the Poet Laureate Sir Andrew Motion who said that the collection stood out for 'the attention the poems pay to their subjects' and 'the range and strangeness of its interests.' In *On Board Arcadia* the lover of the Emperor Hadrian tells his story alongside the piano-playing partner of a Camden Town house clearance dealer; Cosimo Duke of Tuscany shares space with Henri Rousseau's talking cat. An eighteenth century mother grieves for her ruined daughter to William Hogarth while the goddess Demeter looks for her own lost daughter in a Christmas Market in contemporary Rome.

Sue Boyle likes her characters to step out of history, darkness and silence and confide the core truths about their lives without the author getting in the way. Trained to teach drama and creative writing, she writes direct and accessible poems for the voice – or rather for the many voices in the series of short volumes which make up *On Board Arcadia*. A Londoner by family and background, she has lived in ten English counties and worked as a teacher, social worker, antiquarian print dealer, market trader in bric-a-brac and maker of hand-finished picture frames. For the past six years she has organised the Bath Poetry Cafe and the associated Cafe Writing Days.

Arcadia is a world full of surprise and revelation as the poems explore what lies below the surface of the ordinary and bring old histories into the present day. 'Sue Boyle's is the voice of a true original: her work has a wit and inventiveness all too rare in poetry today.' (Rosie Bailey)

On Board Arcadia

A series of six themed short volumes available at readings and workshops or direct from Amazon.

Volume One
A Day Out on the Thames
Twenty-two poems

Against a background of momentous historical events – the fires of the London blitz, the dropping of the atom bomb, the terrors of the Cold War – the poems in *A Day Out on the Thames* focus their affectionate attention on the aspirations and disappointments of one London family: the texture of treasured moments, daily life and familiar places, the complex of memories which becomes the inheritance of those who are left behind. There are sorrows, difficulty, loneliness, and loss, but it is the passion for living and for the wonder of life which the poems celebrate. The collection closes with the serenity of the prize-winning sonnet, 'Thinking About the Swans.'

October 2013
ISBN-13:978-1483961668

Volume Two
Mr Marksbury's Careful Choice of Beds
Twenty-two poems

Mr Marksbury's Careful Choice of Beds is a book about London, but not perhaps the London the tourist knows. One by one, strange characters make their intriguing cameo appearances: Virgil Christopher the living statue; Flavia the poledancer; the lonely collector of vintage glass. We visit a country auction and overnight at a giant antiques fair. We also meet a rescue ferret, a unicorn, a couple of angels and a famous talking cat. From Kew Gardens to Canary Wharf, Camden Town antiques dealer Mr Marksbury makes his way through this offbeat geography, shedding light on dark places and offering his idiosyncratic views on leading the good life. There are also useful lessons on how to fake an old master painting, lie down safely with a lion and recognise true love.

October 2013
ISBN-13:978-1491021880

Volume Three
A Respectable Neighbourhood
Thirty-nine poems

Behind the closed doors of houses, the closed doors of the heart – the secrets, dangers, delights and sorrows of human love. From first encounters to bereavement, with lovers ranging back from the contemporary to the depths of ancient myth, the collection takes its theme from 'A Leisure Centre is Also a Temple of Learning' and explores 'what happens next.' Will we be faithful, unfaithful, cherished, abandoned, blameworthy, innocent? We never know what waits behind the door until we make the frightening commitment to step inside the house of love.

October 2013
ISBN-13: 978-1490946917

Volume Four
Report from the Judenplatz
Nine Lamentations & A Play for Witnesses

The sequence of nine lamentations in *Report from the Judenplatz* is also presented as a play for witnesses to be shared by any number of participants as a way of honouring the victims of the Holocaust. Between 1939 and 1945 most of Europe turned its back on its Jewish citizens. This book tries to hear the voice of those absences – the abiding silence of the streets and squares emptied by the deportations – and to make a space in which to remember the richness of the culture which the Nazi genocide intended to destroy. The cover design is by kind permission of the Yad Vashem Holocaust Memorial and Institute in Jerusalem and profits from the sale of *Report from the Judenplatz* will be donated to the Yad Vashem UK Foundation.

October 2013
ISBN-13:978-1482776294

Volume Five
Ark Music
Twenty-six poems

Ark Music, the fifth volume of *On Board Arcadia*, is a strange, dark collection which explores the belief that man is the intended master of the earth. From the first lobe-finned fish to the last extinction, from the Trojan War to the threat of nuclear armageddon, we are casualties of our species' ambition and belligerence. A grieving celebration of the wonder and beauty of the planet as it turns in its 'cage of stars', the poems in *Ark Music* reach towards a gentler way of being in the world and try to open up a place in imagination for a new 'ark' so that what is left of the precious, varied and fragile might be better cherished and perhaps be saved.

October 2013
ISBN-13:978-1491041772

coming soon

Volume Six
A Small Menagerie

Time & Tide Publishing
London EC1

Made in the USA
Charleston, SC
08 October 2013